NOVELLO
classics
for the flute

J. S. Bach

Suite No.2 in B minor

BWV 1067

Edited by
Trevor Wye
Piano arrangement by
Robert Scott

Novello

Order No. NOV 120767

Trevor Wye studied the flute privately with Geoffrey Gilbert and the celebrated Marcel Moyse. He was a freelance player on the London scene for many years and has made several solo recordings, notably on his specialist instrument, the *flute d'amour*.

He was formerly a Professor at the Guildhall School of Music, London and the Royal Northern College of Music in Manchester. In 1990 he was made a Fellow of the Royal Northern College of Music.

Trevor Wye is the author of the famous *Practice Books*, about all technical aspects of flute playing, which have received world wide acclaim and have been translated into eight other languages. During the year, he teaches at his Studio in Kent and travels throughout the world giving master classes including annual appearances in the USA, UK, Canada, Switzerland, Spain, Italy and Japan. He enjoys serving on international competition juries, giving recitals and presenting his unique *Flutes Fantastic!* – a hilarious lecture recital in which he plays on more than fifty different flutes.

He founded the British Flute Society, the International Summer School and more recently, the Summer Flute Academy.

This popular *Suite* is one of Bach's best known works. Close attention has been given here to authenticity and detailed performance notes are included. The accompaniment has been arranged specifically for piano rather than simply as an orchestral reduction, without sacrificing any essential elements.

Avec introduction en francais
Mit deutscher Einleitung
Con introduzione in italiano

Suite No.2 in B Minor BWV 1067
for Flute, Strings and Continuo

Johann Sebastian Bach was born in Eisenach, Thuringia in 1685. During his life he occupied posts as violinist in the orchestra of a prince, organist, the chief musician of a court, and Cantor of a municipal school. He married twice and had a total of twenty children several of whom became eminent musicians. In 1723 he took up his last position, that of Director of the Collegium Musicum in Leipzig, where he died in 1750.

Bach composed four orchestral *Suites*, the exact chronology of which it is impossible to determine, though it is thought that numbers 1 (BWV 1066) and 4 (BWV 1069) date from the Cöthen period (*c*.1717–1723) and the other two from the late 1730s. It is possible that Bach met the celebrated French Flute virtuoso Pierre-Gabriel Buffardin and wrote the second *Suite* for him, perhaps thinking about him when he wrote the *Badinerie* knowing of Buffardin's agility in fast passages.

It is likely that the French style of composition of the four *Suites* was to satisfy the taste for French music shown by many employers at this time. (Telemann wrote hundreds of orchestral suites of which only 135 are known to survive.)

The *Suite* begins with an *Overture* so obviously in the French mold that no speed indications were thought necessary. The repeat at the end of the *Overture* is seldom taken in today's performances.

The first edition of this famous *Suite* was published in 1853, edited by Hans Von Bülow. As the autograph score no longer existed, Bach's own parts were used: the flute and viola parts were in the composer's own hand and the two violin parts and the continuo part had been corrected by him.

In the nineteenth century, other transcriptions were made for piano solo, and for piano two hands.

Performing notes on this edition

Style[1] As the *Overture* and *Suite* were written in the French style, the rhythms to be performed are not always indicated by the composer. To display all the variants would not be possible as there are a few instances where various ways of performing a particular rhythm is a matter of taste. The general rhythmic style has been indicated: however the performer should play these rhythms in all applicable places.

In the slow sections of the *Overture,* and in the *Sarabande* and *Polonaise,* the dotted rhythms should be 'over dotted' and between the dotted note and its complement, a small 'articulation silence' should be inserted. [See example below]

The use of *inégale,* or uneven rhythm, may enhance some of the *Suite* movements where appropriate, particularly the *Rondeau.*

Ornaments Suggested interpretation of the *appoggiaturas* and *trills* have been printed below the flute part for the guidance of the performer, based on present day informed knowledge; though, in some cases, there will always be disagreement as to exactly the rhythm to be played. It is undoubtedly more important to play the *appoggiaturas* in the right

spirit, that is to say, always *diminuendo* from the principal note to its resolution.

Extra trills can be added when appropriate; a few suggestions have been indicated.

Speeds Suggested speeds have been added in brackets where there were none marked by the composer. The *Overture* – which has no speed indication – should not be played too slowly.

Piano part As most performances are for flute and piano, the piano part in this edition is a transcription of the score *arranged for piano* and not simply an orchestral reduction. The right hand of the keyboard has been made as playable as possible without sacrificing the essential harmony or melodic turns of phrase in the string parts. Where the first violin part doubles that of the flute, which occurs through much of the *Suite,* it has been largely omitted from the accompaniment. This of course places a limitation on the melodic interest of the keyboard part. However, the bass line in itself holds sufficient interest for the player, whose right hand should be kept relatively soft and light if a piano is used, particularly in the faster movements.

Trevor Wye and Robert Scott, 1995

1) A reliable book should be consulted such as *The Interpretation of Early Music* by Robert Donnington (Faber and Faber).
   A brief introduction to early music is Thurston Dart's *The Interpretation of Music* (Hutchinson).

Suite No.2 en si mineur (BWV 1067)

Johann Sebastian Bach est né à Eisenach, en Thuringe, en 1685. Il remplit, à diverses époques de sa vie, les fonctions de violoniste dans l'orchestre d'un prince, d'organiste, de directeur musical d'une cour princière et de Cantor d'une école municipale. Il se maria deux fois et eut vingt enfants dont certains devinrent d'éminents musiciens. En 1723, il fut nommé à son dernier poste, celui de Directeur du Collegium Musicum de la ville de Leipzig, dans laquelle il mourut en 1750.

Bach composa quatre *Suites* orchestrales dont il est impossible de déterminer l'exacte chronologie. On pense cependant que les *Suites No 1* (BWV 1066) et *4* (BWV 1069) remontent à l'époque de Cöthen (env. 1717–1723) et que les deux autres datent de la fin des années 1730. Peut-être Bach a-t-il rencontré le célèbre flûtiste virtuose français Pierre-Gabriel Buffardin et écrit la deuxième *Suite* pour lui en pensant à l'agilité de Buffardin dans les mouvements rapides pour la *Badinerie*.

Le style français des quatre *Suites* était, selon toute vraisemblance, destiné à satisfaire le goût manifesté par de nombreux commanditaires de cette époque pour la musique française. (Telemann écrivit des centaines de suites orchestrales dont seules 135 sont connues.)

La *Suite* commence par une *Overture* si évidemment sortie du moule français qu'aucune indication de tempo ne s'y avérait nécessaire. La reprise à la fin de l'*Overture* est rarement effectuée lors des exécutions actuelles.

La première édition de cette célèbre *Suite*, due à Hans von Bülow, fut publiée en 1853. La partition autographe ayant disparu, on l'établit à partir des parties séparées de Bach lui-même: les parties de flûte et d'alto transcrites de la main du compositeur et les deux parties de violon ainsi que la basse continue corrigées par lui.

Au XIXe siècle, d'autres transcriptions furent réalisées pour piano seul et pour piano à quatre mains.

Notes sur l'exécution de cette édition

Style[1] L'*Overture* et la *Suite* étant composées dans le style français, le compositeur n'a pas toujours précisé les rythmes à exécuter. La notation de toutes les variantes rythmiques est impossible dans la mesure où, dans certains cas, les différentes interprétations d'un rythme demeurent une question de goût. Le style rythmique général a été indiqué. Toutefois, l'interprète reproduira les rythmes dans les séquences identiques.

Dans les sections lentes de l'*Overture* ainsi que dans la *Sarabande* et dans la *Polonaise*, les rythmes pointés seront 'surpointés' et un bref 'silence d'articulation' sera inséré entre la note pointée et sa note complémentaire. [Voir l'exemple ci-dessous]

Le recours aux notes inégales, dans les passages qui s'y prêtent, mettra en valeur certains mouvements de la *Suite*, en particulier le *Rondeau*.

Ornements Une suggestion d'exécution des *appoggiatures* et des *trilles* figure en dessous de la partie de flûte afin de guider l'interprète en fonction des connaissances actuelles. Cependant, des désaccords subsisteront, dans certains cas, quant au rythme exact à exécuter. Il est, sans nul doute, plus important de jouer les *appoggiatures* selon l'esprit juste, c'est-à-dire toujours *diminuendo* à partir de la note

principale vers sa résolution. Quelques *trilles* supplémentaires, dont l'ajout se révèle opportun, ont été signalés.

Tempos Des tempos sont proposés entre parenthèses lorsque aucun mouvement n'a été spécifié par le compositeur. L'*Overture* – qui ne comporte aucune indication de mouvement – ne doit pas être jouée trop lentement.

Partie de piano La plupart des exécutions associant flûte et piano, la partie de piano de cette édition est un *arrangement pour le piano* de la partition et non une simple réduction orchestrale. La main droite du clavier a été traitée sans sacrifier ni l'harmonie fondamentale, ni les contours mélodiques des parties de cordes. En cas de doublure de la partie de flûte par celle du premier violon – occurrence fréquente tout au long de la *Suite* – cette dernière a été largement supprimée de l'accompagnement. Ceci, bien entendu, réduit l'intérêt mélodique de la partie de clavier. Toutefois, la ligne de basse se révèle, en elle-même, suffisamment attachante pour l'instrumentiste qui devra atténuer et alléger sa main droite, notamment dans les mouvements rapides, s'il joue au piano.

Trevor Wye et Robert Scott, 1995
(Traduction Agnès Ausseur)

1) On consultera à ce sujet l'ouvrage documenté de Robert DONNINGTON, *The Interpretation of Early Music* (Faber & Faber) ainsi que la brève introduction à la musique ancienne de Thurston DART, *The Interpretation of Music* (Hutchinson).

Suite No.2 in H-Moll (BWV 1067)

Johann Sebastian Bach wurde 1685 in Eisenach (Thüringen) geboren. Er hatte Stellen als Violinist im Orchester eines Prinzen, Organist, Hofkapellmeister und Kantor an einer städtischen Schule inne. Er war zweimal verheiratet und hatte zwanzig Kinder, von denen einige berühmte Musiker wurden. 1723 trat er seine letzte Stelle als Direktor des Collegium Musicum in Leipzig an, wo er 1750 starb.

Bach komponierte vier *Orchestersuiten.* Ihre Chronologie läßt sich nicht genau festlegen. Vermutlich stammen die Nummern 1 (BWV 1066) und 4 (BWV 1069) aus der Köthener Zeit (c. 1717–1723) und die beiden anderen aus den späten 1730er Jahren. Es ist möglich, daß Bach den berühmten französischen Flötenvirtuosen Pierre-Gabriel Buffardin traf und die zweite *Suite* für ihn schrieb. Er dachte mög-licherweise an Buffardin, der für sein müheloses Spiel schneller Musik bekannt war, als er die *Badinerie* schrieb.

Möglicherweise sollte der französische Kompositionsstil der vier Suiten die Vorliebe für französische Musik befriedigen, die viele Dienstherren zu jener Zeit hegten. (Telemann schrieb hunderte Orchestersuiten, von denen uns nur 135 überliefert sind.)

Die *Suite* beginnt mit einer *Ouvertüre*, die so typisch französisch ist, daß Bach es nicht für nötig hielt, Tempoangaben einzutragen. Die Wiederholung am Ende der *Ouvertüre* wird in heutigen Aufführungen selten gespielt.

Diese berühmte *Suite* wurde erstmals 1853 veröffentlicht, bearbeitet von Hans von Bülow. Da das Autograph der Partitur nicht mehr vorhanden ist, wurden Bachs eigene Stimmen verwendet: die Flöten- und Violastimmen in der Handschrift des Komponisten sowie die beiden Violinstimmen und der Generalbaßteil mit Bachs Änderungen.

Im neunzehnten Jahrhundert wurden andere Übertragungen für Soloklavier angefertigt, sowie für Klavier zu zwei Händen.

Aufführungsanmerkungen zu dieser Ausgabe

Stil[1] Da die *Ouvertüre* und *Suite* im französischen Stil geschrieben worden waren, gab der Komponist nicht immer die zu verwendenden Rhythmen an. Es ist nicht möglich, alle Varianten aufzuführen, da es einige Fälle gibt, in denen die Wahl einer bestimmten Aufführungsart eines Rhythmus Geschmackssache ist. Der allgemeine rhythmische Stil wurde angedeutet: der Ausführende sollte diese Rhythmen jedoch an den parallelen Stellen spielen.

Im langsameren Teil der *Ouvertüre* sowie in der *Sarabande* und *Polonaise* sollten die punktierten Rhythmen '*stark punktiert*' werden und zwischen der punktierten Note und ihrer Ergänzung sollte eine kurze 'Artikulationspause' eingefügt werden. [Beispiel unten]

Der Gebrauch von *inégale* oder ungleichmäßigen Rhythmen mag, wo angemessen, die Wirkung einiger Suitesätze steigern, besonders das *Rondeau*.

Verzierungen Empfohlene Interpretationen der *Vorschläge* und *Triller* wurden unter dem Flötenteil zur Orientierung des Ausführenden gedruckt und basieren auf unserem heutigen Wissen, obwohl es in einigen Fällen immer Meinungsverschiedenheiten bezüglich des zu spielenden Rhythmus geben wird. Es ist zweifellos wichtiger, die *Vorschläge* im richtigen Geist zu spielen, das heißt, immer *diminuendo* von der Hauptnote zu ihrer Auflösung.

Zusätzliche *Triller* können, wenn nötig, hinzugefügt werden; einige Vorschläge wurden angedeutet.

Geschwindigkeit Empfohlene Geschwindigkeiten wurden dort in Klammern hinzugefügt, wo der Komponist keine eingetragen hatte. Die *Ouvertüre*, die keine Tempoangaben enthält, sollte nicht zu langsam gespielt werden.

Klavierteil Da die meisten Aufführungen für Flöte und Klavier sind, ist der Klavierteil in dieser Ausgabe eine Übertragung der Partitur *arrangiert für Klavier* und nicht ein bloßer Klavierauszug. Die Stimme in der rechten Hand des Pianisten wurde so spielbar wie möglich gemacht ohne Preisgabe der wesentlichen Harmonie oder der melodischen Phrasierungen in den Streichern. An den Stellen, wo die erste Violinstimme die Flöte verdoppelt, was in einem großen Teil der *Suite* der Fall ist, wurde sie meistens aus der Begleitung weggelassen. Dies führt selbstverständlich zu einer Einschränkung des melodischen Interesses des Klavierteils. Die Baßstimme ist jedoch selbst von genügend Interesse für den Spieler – dessen rechte Hand relativ weich und leicht sein sollte — wenn ein Klavier verwendet wird, besonders in den schnelleren Sätzen.

Trevor Wye und Robert Scott, 1995
(Übers. Gunhild Lenz-Mulligan)

Geschrieben / Gespielt

1) Ein verläßliches Werk sollte zu Rate gezogen werden, wie zum Beispiel THE INTERPRETATION OF EARLY MUSIC von Robert Donnington (Faber and Faber).
Thurston Darts THE INTERPRETATION OF MUSIC (Hutchinson) gibt eine kurze Einführung zu früher Musik.

Suite N 2 in Si Minore (BWV 1067)

Johann Sebastian Bach nacque ad Eisenach in Turingia nel 1685. Nel corso della sua vita egli fu violinista nell' orchestra di un principe, organista, musicista capo di corte e Cantor di una scuola municipale. Si sposò due volte ed ebbe in tutto venti figli, alcuni dei quali divennero rinomati musicisti. Nel 1723 prese possesso del suo ultimo incarico, quello di direttore del Collegium Musicum di Lipsia, dove morì nel 1750.

Bach compose quattro *Suite* per orchestra la cui cronologia è impossibile determinare esattamente, anche se si crede che la numero 1 (BWV 1066) e numero 4 (BWV 1069) appartengano al periodo di Cöthen (ca 1717–23) e le altre due alla fine degli anni 1730.

È possibile che Bach abbia incontrato il francese Pierre-Gabriel Buffardin, celebre virtuoso di flauto, e composto la seconda *Suite*, e la *Badinerie* in particolare, per lui, ricordando la sua agilità nei passaggi veloci.

È probabile che lo stile francese delle quattro suite intendesse soddisfare il diffuso gusto francese dei committenti di quell' epoca. (Telemann scrisse centinaia di suite per orchestra di cui si pensa che soltanto 135 ci siano rimaste.)

La *Suite* inizia con un *Overture* così chiaramente francesizzante che si creduto superfluo dare un indicazione di velocità. Il ritornello alla fine dell' *Overture* è raramente eseguito nelle esecuzioni dei nostri giorni.

La prima edizione di questa *Suite* fu pubblicata da Hans von Bülow nel 1853. Poichè l'originale della partitura non esisteva più, si usarono le parti di Bach stesso: quella del flauto e della viola erano di mano del compositore, quelle dei due violini e del continuo erano state corrette da lui stesso.

Nel diciannovesimo secolo furono fatte altre trascrizione per pianoforte solo e per pianoforte a quattro mani.

Note di esecuzione a questa edizione

Stile [1] Poichè l'*Overture* e la *Suite* furono scritte nello stile francese, i ritmi da eseguire non sono sempre quelli indicati dal compositore. Proporre tutte le varianti non sarebbe possibile essendo in vari casi la scelta del modo di esecuzione una questione di gusto.

Gli andamenti ritmici di massima sono stati indicati e devono essere applicati nei ritorni degli stessi materiali.

Nelle sezioni lente dell'*Overture*, nella *Sarabanda* e nella *Polonaise* le note puntate devono essere eseguite con doppio o triplo punto e tra la nota puntata e il suo completamento si deve inserire un breve silenzio di articolazione. [Vedi esempio sotto]

L'uso dell' ineguaglianza, *notes inégales*, può migliorare se usata in modo appropriato l'esecuzione di alcuni movimenti della *Suite*, in particolare il *Rondeau*.

Ornamentazione Un consiglio per l'interpretazione delle *appoggiature* e dei *trilli* è stato stampato sotto la parte del flauto come guida per l'esecutore. Ci si è basati sulle più verificate teorie correnti anche se in alcuni casi ci sarà sempre disaccordo su l'esatto ritmo da suonare. Comunque è senz'altro la cosa più importante che le *appoggiature* siano eseguite con il giusto spirito, cioè in *diminuendo*

dalla nota principale alla sua risoluzione. Qualche trillo può essere aggiunto dove appropriato; si sono dati alcuni suggerimenti.

Velocità I suggerimenti di velocità sono aggiunti in parentesi quando manca un indicazione del compositore. L'*Overture* – che non ha indicazione di velocità – non deve essere eseguita troppo lentamente.

Parte del pianoforte Poichè la maggior parte delle esecuzioni avviene con pianoforte e flauto, la parte del pianoforte è una trascrizione di un *arrangiamento per piano* della partitura piuttosto che una mera riduzione pianistica della stessa. Si è cercato di rendere la mano destra il più pianistica possibile senza sacrificare l'armonia o gli andamenti melodici specifici della scrittura degli archi. Quando la parte dei primi violini raddoppia quella del flauto, il che accade in quasi tutta la *Suite*, la si è per lo più tralasciata anche se questo comporta una riduzione dell'interesse melodico dell'accompagnamento. La linea del basso offre comunque abbastanza interesse all'esecutore che dovrà fare un uso della mano destra discreto e relativamente leggero, particolarmente nei movimenti veloci.

Trevor Wye e Robert Scott, 1995
(trans. Luigi Suvini)

1) Si faccia riferimento ad un affidabile testo quale *The Interpretation of Early Music* di Robert Donnington (Faber and Faber).
   Per una breve introduzione alla musica antica si veda *The Interpretation of Music* di Thurston Dart (Hutchinson).

Ouverture & Suite
in B minor

Edited by Trevor Wye

J.S. BACH

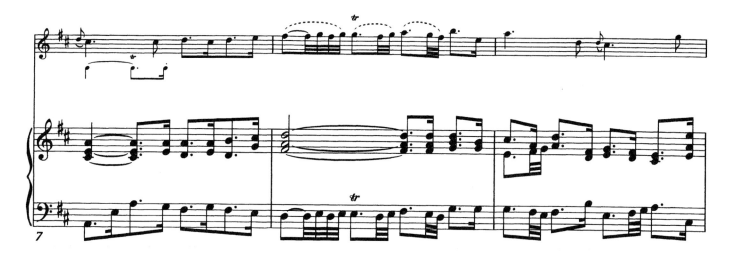

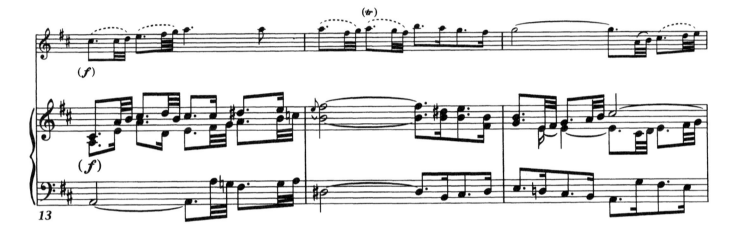

40

44

48

52

5

57

62

67

72

C

111

115

119

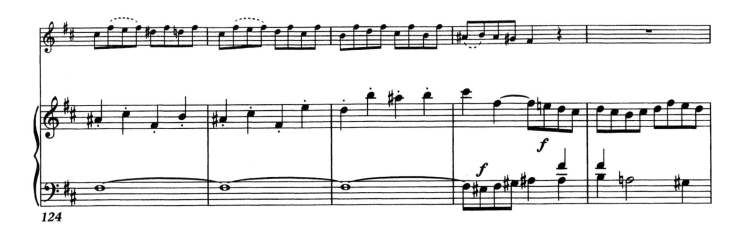

124

129

133

138

142

146

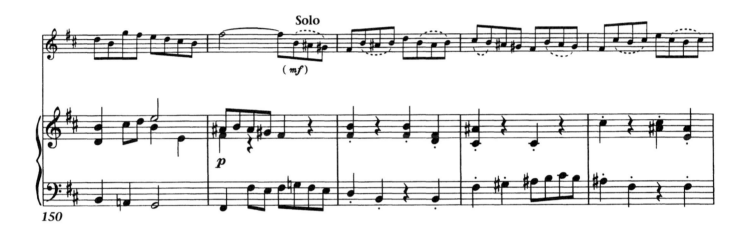

150

155

160

184

188

192

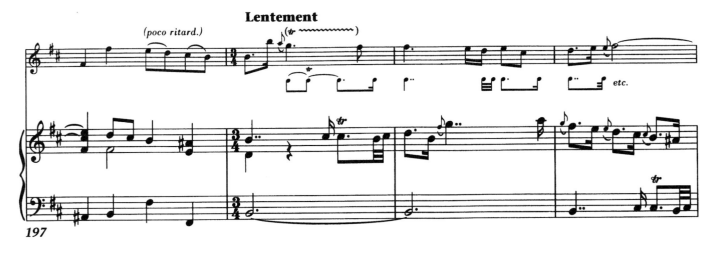

197

SUITE

Rondeau (♩ = *c.* 60)

Sarabande

(**Andante** ♩ = *c.* 68)

7

13

19

25

29

Bourrée I. Alternativement

(Allegro ♩= c. 92)

7

Bourrée II
Doucement

Polonaise

Lentement (♩= *c.* 50)

Double

Polonaise D.C.

Menuet
(♩ = c. 96)

7

13

19

Badinerie

(♩ = c. 104-108)

6

12

17

22

26

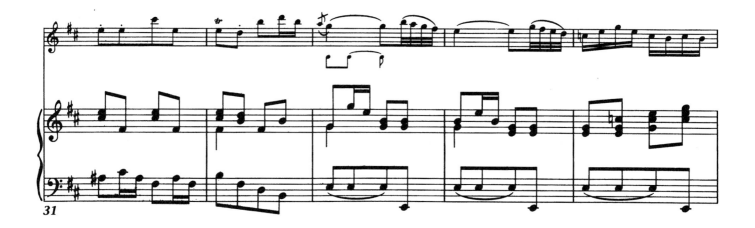

31

36

Published by Novello Publishing Limited
Music set by Stave Origination

NOV120767

Ouverture & Suite
in B minor

Edited by Trevor Wye

J.S. BACH

FLUTE

FLUTE

97

102

107

113

119

124

133

139

145

151

Suite

Sarabande
(Andante ♩= c.68)

Bourrée I. Alternativement
(Allegro ♩= c.92)

Bourrée II
Doucement

Bourrée I D.C

Polonaise

Double

Menuet

Badinerie
($\quarternote$ = *c.* 104-108)

Published by Novello Publishing Limited
Music setting by Stave Origination